Adventures With The Prophets Stories For Young Hearts

To all the curious hearts and giggling adventurers out there

May these stories light up your imagination,

tickle your funny bone,

and remind you that even the smallest hero can

have the biggest adventure.

And to every grown-up reading this aloud

Thanks for making storytime magical.

Now, let's dive in—adventures await!

Book Cover by Tukotuku Publishing

Illustrations by Tukotuku Publishing

First edition 2025

Print ISBN: 978-1-991339-43-0

Ebook ISBN: 978-1-991339-44-7

TU
KO
TU
KU PUBLISHING

Contents

Welcome to Adventures with the Prophets

Stories for Young Hearts

Hey there, young adventurer! Welcome to a book jam-packed with stories so amazing, so thrilling, and sometimes so funny, you'll wonder why Hollywood hasn't made blockbuster movies about them yet. Grab your snack (preferably not fish sticks—you'll understand why in Chapter 1) and get cozy, because we're about to dive headfirst into some of the coolest tales ever told.

But first, let's set some ground rules:

1. **No skipping ahead!** Trust me, every story is worth the wait.

2. **Feel free to laugh out loud.** Prophets were wise, brave, and kind—but some-

times, their adventures were straight-up hilarious.

3. **Snacks are encouraged.** (Just maybe not popcorn during the Jonah chapter—you'll see why.)

Now, you might be wondering, "What's this book all about, anyway?" Great question! This isn't just any book—it's a treasure map to some of the most inspiring, heartwarming, and occasionally fishy stories from Islamic history. Each chapter introduces you to a different prophet and their unique, wild, and sometimes downright bonkers adventure.

You'll meet Jonah, who tried to run away from his responsibilities and ended up in a giant fish's belly (imagine that on a vacation postcard). You'll chill with Prophet Nuh (Noah), the original zookeeper-slash-boat captain, and hear how he built the biggest floating petting zoo ever. And let's not forget Musa (Moses), who had a magical staff cooler than any superhero gadget.

But these aren't just action-packed tales with plot twists that could rival your favorite cartoons—they're also packed with lessons. No, no, don't groan yet. These aren't the boring, "sit up straight, eat your broccoli" kind of lessons. These are life lessons, the kind that stick with you long after the book closes. Lessons about bravery, kindness, patience, and trusting in something bigger than yourself.

Oh, and did I mention animals? There are so many animals. Big ones, little ones, flying ones, swimming ones—honestly, it's like an all-you-can-read animal adventure buffet.

And here's the best part: you don't need to memorize anything or write a book report at the end. All you have to do is relax, turn the pages, and enjoy the ride. Think of me as your story guide—part narrator, part jokester, and part snack enthusiast.

Whether you're reading this at bedtime, on a long car ride, or sneakily under your blanket with a flashlight when you're supposed to be sleeping (I see you!), these stories are here to keep you company.

So, are you ready to meet some incredible prophets, learn

some timeless lessons, and maybe—just maybe—giggle at a few unexpected plot twists along the way?

Good! Buckle up, buttercup. The adventure begins now, and trust me—you don't want to miss a single page.

Now flip on over to Chapter 1, and let's get this adventure started! (P.S. Watch out for any giant fish.)

A Whale of a Tale

Jonah and the Big Fish

O nce upon a time, in a land far, far away, there lived a prophet named Jonah. Jonah was a bit like a superhero, but instead of a cape, he wore a heart full of kindness and a mind full of adventure. One day, God told Jonah to go to a big city called Nineveh to help the people there, who were not behaving very nicely. But Jonah thought, "Hmm, that sounds like a lot of work! What if I just took a little vacation instead?" And with that idea, he hopped on a ship sailing in the opposite direction. Spoiler alert: this vacation wasn't going to go as planned!

As Jonah was sailing away, the weather suddenly changed. The sky turned dark and the waves began to dance like a wild party! The sailors on the ship were scared and started throwing things overboard. They were shouting, "Help! We're going to sink!" Meanwhile,

Jonah was taking a nice nap below deck. When the captain found him, he exclaimed, "Wake up! We need your help!" Jonah rubbed his eyes and realized that his little vacation was turning into a big disaster. So, he told the sailors, "I think this storm is my fault. Just throw me overboard, and you'll be safe!" The sailors were not too thrilled about this idea, but they did what Jonah said.

As Jonah splashed into the ocean, he must have thought he was in a fishy situation. Suddenly, a gigantic fish swam up and gulped him down like a big spaghetti noodle!

Inside the fish, Jonah had lots of time to think. He realized that running away from God's plan was not the best choice. "What a weird hotel this is," he joked to himself. "No room service, and the décor is all slimy!" After three days and nights of thinking and praying inside the fish, Jonah decided it was time to make things right.

Finally, the fish got a little tummyache and decided to spit Jonah out onto dry land. "Phew! That was one fishy ride!" Jonah exclaimed as he landed with a thud. Now, Jonah was ready to do what God asked him to do. He made his way to Nineveh and told the people, "Hey, you need to change your ways!" To his surprise, the people listened! They were so impressed that they decided to be better. Jonah was amazed and thought, "Wow, maybe I should have taken a vacation in Nineveh after all!"

In the end, Jonah learned a valuable lesson: it's always better to follow God's plans than to swim away from them. Even though his adventure was a little fishy, it taught him and the people of Nineveh to be kind and to listen. So, whenever you see a fish, remember Jonah's big adventure and think about how important it is to follow the right path. And if you ever find yourself in a tricky situation, just remember that a good attitude can turn even the biggest problems into funny stories!

Lessons from the Deep

In the vast ocean of stories, there lived a fish named Finny who loved to explore. Finny was not just any fish; he had a bright yellow tail that sparkled like the sun. One day, while swimming near a coral reef, Finny overheard a group of sea creatures chatting about the wise old octopus named Ollie. They said Ollie knew everything about the ocean and could teach them important lessons. Finny's fins fluttered with excitement. "I must find Ollie and learn some wisdom!" he declared, puffing out his chest like a little superhero.

After swimming through a seaweed forest and dodging jellyfish that tickled his fins, Finny finally found Ollie. The octopus was lounging in a cozy cave, surrounded by colorful shells. "Hey, Ollie!" Finny shouted, "Can you tell me something important that I need to know?" Ollie chuckled, his tentacles swirling like spaghetti.

"Well, little fish, the first lesson is to always be curious! The ocean is full of wonders, and if you ask questions, you'll discover amazing things!" Finny's eyes widened as he imagined all the mysterious treasures waiting to be found.

Feeling inspired, Finny decided to ask about the second lesson. "Ollie, what else should I know?" With a twinkle in his eye, Ollie replied, "Friendship is key! Just like how I need my tentacles to swim, you need friends to help you navigate through life. Remember to share, care, and sometimes even share a snack!" Finny giggled, thinking about how he could share his favorite seaweed chips with his buddies. He realized that friendship made every adventure more exciting, especially when snacks were involved!

As they continued their chat, Finny couldn't resist asking for one more lesson. "What's the final secret to being awesome, Ollie?" The wise octopus smiled and said, "Always believe in yourself! Just because you're small doesn't mean you can't make a big splash. Even the tiniest fish can have the biggest dreams!" Finny felt a rush of confidence. He imagined himself leading a parade of fish, all dancing and twirling through the water. "I can do anything!" he exclaimed, feeling as mighty as a whale!

With a heart full of lessons from Ollie, Finny swam back to his friends, eager to share his newfound wisdom. "Guess what, everyone! We need to be curious, value our friendships, and believe in ourselves!" His friends cheered and wiggled their fins in excitement. They all agreed to embark on new adventures together, exploring the ocean and making memories. And just like that,

Finny and his friends learned that the deep sea held not just treasures, but also important lessons about life, friendship, and believing in themselves.

The Feathered Friends

Prophet Suleiman and the Talking Birds

O nce upon a time, in a land far, far away, there lived a very special prophet named Suleiman. He was not just any prophet; he was the king of the jinn, humans, and animals! But what made him super-duper special was his ability to talk to birds. Imagine walking into a park and chatting with a parrot about the weather or asking a sparrow what it had for breakfast! That's exactly what Suleiman did, making him the coolest bird-watcher in the history of bird-watching!

One sunny day, Suleiman decided to throw a grand picnic for all his feathered friends. He called the birds from every corner of the kingdom. There were colorful parrots, wise owls, and even chatty pigeons who loved to gossip! As they all gathered, Suleiman said, "Let's have a contest! The bird that tells the funniest joke gets a delicious seed treat!" The birds flapped their wings in excitement, and it was time for some feathered fun!

The first contestant was a cheeky parrot named Polly. She wiggled her feathers and squawked, "Why did the bird get a ticket? Because it was using its wings in the wrong way!" Everyone burst into laughter; even the serious-looking owls couldn't help but chuckle. Next up was a wise old owl who said, "What do you call a bird that can fix anything? A duck tape!" The crowd went wild, flapping their wings and chirping with joy. Suleiman was laughing so hard that he almost dropped his picnic basket!

But then, a little sparrow named Squeaky, who was known for being shy, stepped up. Everyone went silent, curious about what this tiny bird would say. "Why don't birds use Facebook?" Squeaky squeaked nervously. "Because they already have Twitter!" The whole crowd erupted into laughter! Suleiman was so impressed that he declared Squeaky the winner. "You've got a talent for jokes, little friend! Here's your special seed treat!"

As the sun began to set, Suleiman and the birds shared stories, laughter, and yummy food. Just think about it! A prophet, a king, and a bunch of talking birds having a picnic together! This delightful day reminded everyone that friendship and laughter are the best treasures of all. So, whenever you hear a bird chirping, remember that they might just have a funny story or two waiting to be told!

A Day in the Life of a Bird Whisperer

Waking up early in the morning is a special treat for a bird whisperer. As the sun peeks through the curtains, our bird whisperer, Amina, stretches her arms wide like a bird ready to take flight. She hops out of bed, excited to greet her feathery friends. "Good morning, world!" she chirps, and her pet parrot, Zuzu, squawks back, "Good morning, Amina! Can I have pancakes?" Amina giggles, knowing Zuzu might not be able to eat pancakes, but she sure can toss a few crumbs his way!

After breakfast, Amina puts on her favorite bird-patterned scarf and heads outside with a pocket full of birdseed. She loves to visit the park, where the trees are filled with all kinds of chirping, flapping, and hopping birds. As she walks, she practices her best bird sounds. "Tweet-tweet!

Caw-caw!" The squirrels stop and stare, thinking she's lost her mind. But Amina just smiles, knowing that the birds will hear her and come for a visit soon. She even pretends to be a bird herself, flapping her arms and pretending to land on branches. "Look at me! I'm a majestic eagle!" she declares, causing a nearby crow to caw in laughter.

Soon, Amina finds a cozy spot under a big oak tree. She spreads out her picnic blanket and lays out her birdseed like it's a grand feast. "Come and get it, everyone!" she calls. Within moments, a flock of colorful finches, cheer-ful sparrows, and even a shy lit-tle bluebird flit down to join her. Amina talks to them about her day, sharing stories about school, her friends, and even her favorite ice cream flavor. The birds seem to listen, their tiny heads bobbing as if they understand every word. "And that's why chocolate chip mint is the best!" she concludes, and the birds chirp in agreement, or maybe they just want more seeds.

As the sun begins to set, Amina decides it's time to head home. But just as she stands up, a little robin hops closer, looking at her with big, curious eyes. "Oh, you want to come with me?" Amina laughs. "I bet my mom would love a feathered guest!" The robin tilts its head, as if considering the offer. "Just remember to mind your manners at the dinner table!" she jokes, and the robin fluffs its feathers, clearly debating if it could master the art of eating spaghetti.

Back at home, Amina shares her bird adventures with her family over dinner. Zuzu, the parrot, squawks, "Amina, bird whisperer!" and everyone bursts into laughter. Amina smiles, knowing that being a bird whisperer is about more than just talking to birds; it's about understanding and caring for all of Allah's creations. As she finishes her meal, she dreams of tomorrow's adventures, wondering what new friends she will meet and what stories she can share with her feathery pals. With a heart full of joy and a belly full of food, Amina drifts off to sleep, ready to whisper sweet dreams to the birds in her dreams.

Eating with Nature's Best

O nce upon a time, in a land filled with delicious fruits and colorful vegetables, there lived a group of friends who had the best idea ever: to have a picnic with all of nature's tasty treasures! They decided to gather everything they could from the garden and the forest, turning their picnic into a feast fit for a little prophet! But guess what? They didn't just want to eat; they wanted to learn how to eat the way nature intended, and that made them giggle with excitement.

First, they visited the garden where Sammy the Squirrel was busy nibbling on a crunchy carrot. "Hey, Sammy! Can we have some of those?" they called out. Sammy looked up, his cheeks stuffed full. "Sure! But only if you promise to share!" The kids laughed and agreed. They learned that sharing is just as important as eating, especially when it comes to enjoying nature's best. After filling their baskets with carrots, radishes, and even some golden corn, they headed to the forest to find some fruits.

In the forest, they stumbled upon Bella the Bird, who was singing a beautiful song while hopping around a tree full of juicy apples. "Bella, can we pick some apples?" they asked. Bella flapped her wings and chirped, "Of course! Just remember to be kind to the tree and only take what you need." The kids giggled at her wise advice and carefully picked the apples. They learned that nature gives us plenty, but we must always respect it. After all, no one wants a grumpy apple tree!

As they set up their picnic blanket, they realized they had a special guest: Mr. Bumblebee! Buzzing around, he said, "You kids are going to have a great feast! But remember, I help flowers bloom, so please don't forget to thank Allah for all this yummy food!" The kids nodded, their mouths watering. They learned that every bite they take is a blessing, a gift from Allah, and it's good manners to say thank you. So they all shouted together, "Thank you, Allah!" and even did a little happy dance.

Finally, with their picnic underway, they munched on their colorful feast and laughed until their bellies hurt. They shared stories about the prophets and how they loved the gifts of nature too. They realized that eating with nature's best isn't just about filling their tummies; it's about friendship, respect, and gratitude. And so, every time they took a bite, they made sure to remember the lessons of sharing, kindness, and thankfulness. Who knew that eating could be such a fun adventure?

The Amazing Ark Adventure

Prophet Nuh and His Floating Zoo

Once upon a time, in a land filled with tall mountains and deep rivers, there lived a very special man named Prophet Nuh. Now, Prophet Nuh was not just any ordinary guy; he was someone with a big heart and an even bigger job. You see, he had a mission from Allah to build a gigantic boat called an Ark. And not just any boat—this Ark would be the ultimate floating zoo! Imagine a boat so big that it could hold every animal you could ever think of, from roaring lions to hopping kangaroos. Talk about a wild party!

One sunny day, as Prophet Nuh was hammering away at his Ark, the people in his town gathered around. They were scratching their heads, whispering, and chuckling. "What's he doing?" one person asked. "Building a boat? On dry land? He must be out of his mind!" They laughed and poked fun at him, but Prophet Nuh just smiled and kept working. He knew something they didn't: a big surprise was coming! Meanwhile, the animals were getting excited, too! Can you picture a giraffe trying to sneak a peek over the boat's edge while a parrot squawked, "Are we there yet?"

As the days turned into weeks, and the weeks into months, the Ark slowly took shape. It was like a giant floating playground! There were slides made from rainbows and swings made from clouds—okay, maybe not, but you get the idea! The animals started arriving two by two. "Hurry up, sloths!" shouted the birds, who were flapping their wings in excitement. The elephants trumpeted, "Make way for the big guys!" It was a hilarious scene as all the animals jostled for space. Who knew that building a zoo could be so much fun?

Then, one day, the sky turned gray and dark clouds rolled in. The people who had laughed at Prophet Nuh started to worry. They looked at the sky and then at the Ark. "Uh-oh! Maybe we should have listened to him!" they exclaimed. But it was too late. The rain began to pour, and soon the whole land was covered in water. The Ark floated higher and higher, with all the animals safely inside. While the townsfolk scrambled for shelter, inside the Ark, it was a party! "Who ordered the rain dance?" laughed the monkeys as they swung from the rafters while the penguins slid around like they were on ice.

After many days of floating, the rain finally stopped, and the sun peeked out from behind the clouds. Prophet Nuh opened the door of the Ark, and out came the animals, leaping and bounding onto dry land. "What an adventure!" the lion roared. "I'm going to tell my friends about the time I went on a boat ride with a bunch of silly animals!" And Prophet Nuh smiled, knowing that his floating zoo had not only saved the animals but had also taught everyone a valuable lesson about faith, patience, and listening to the truth. So, whenever you see a rainbow after the rain, remember the amazing story of Prophet Nuh and his floating zoo!

A Splash of Fun

Animals on Board

Imagine you're on a big, beautiful boat, sailing across a sparkling sea. The sun is shining, and the waves are dancing! But wait! What's that? A bunch of animals have decided to join you on this amazing adventure! Yes, you heard it right. It's not just you and your friends on this boat; it's a whole crew of funny animals ready to make your journey un-forgettable.

First, there's Ali the parrot, who thinks he's the captain of the ship! He squawks, "Polly wants a crack-er!" every time you try to give him directions. Instead of steer-ing the boat, he's busy mimicking everyone's voices. "Oh, Captain Ali, why don't you let me steer?" you might ask. And he'll reply, "Steer? I thought we were here to have a party!" He loves to sing sil-ly songs, and before you know it, everyone on board is dancing like a bunch of jellybeans!

Next, we meet Fatima the fox, who is an expert in hide-and-seek. She sneaks off and hides behind barrels, and when you finally find her, she jumps out and shouts, "Surprise!" But, Fatima's so good at hiding that she accidentally hid herself in a barrel full of apples! Now, instead of just one fox, you've got a Fatima apple pie! Everyone bursts into laughter while Fatima tries to shake off the apples, looking like a fruity superhero.

Then there's Malik the monkey, who thinks he's a clown! He swings from the ropes, throws bananas at everyone, and tells the silliest jokes. "Why did the banana go to the doctor?" he asks with a cheeky grin. When you say you don't know, he swings closer and cackles, "Because it wasn't peeling well!" The laughter echoes across the sea, making the dolphins jump and play along, as if they're joining in the fun.

As the day winds down, all the animals gather around to share their favorite stories. They talk about the wonders of creation, the beautiful animals Allah has made, and the lessons they've learned from the Prophets. With every tale, the boat rocks gently on the waves, and you can almost feel the love and laughter filling the air. You realize that each animal, just like you, has a special role on this adventure, reminding you that life is about sharing joy, respect, and a little bit of silliness along the way.

Fireproof Friends

Prophet Ibrahim and the Fiery Challenge

In a far away land, there lived a man named Ibrahim, who was as brave as a lion and as wise as an owl. Now, Ibrahim had a big job: he was a prophet, which means he got special messages from Allah, the one and only God. But not everyone in his town was happy about this. Some people thought it was a silly idea to worship one God instead of many. Imagine telling your friends that you only like one flavor of ice cream when there are so many to choose from! That's how strange it felt to them. But Ibrahim stood tall, determined to share the truth, even when it was tough.

One day, the king of the land, who was known for being grumpy like a bear that just woke up from a nap, decided that he didn't like Ibrahim's message at all. He was so angry that he thought, "Let's teach this Ibrahim a lesson!" So, he ordered a huge bonfire to be built. It was the biggest fire you could ever imagine—flames reaching up to the sky like they were trying to tickle the clouds! Ibrahim, however, was as cool as a cucumber. He knew that Allah was always with him, and he wasn't scared at all. In fact, he might have even thought it was a little funny, like a wild game of peek-a-boo with the flames.

When the fiery challenge was ready, the king had Ibrahim tossed into the fire. But here's the funny part: instead of getting burned, Ibrahim found himself sitting in a cozy little spot with fluffy clouds and cool breezes all around him. It was like having a picnic in the park! The fire turned into a friendly campfire, and instead of frightening flames, there were twinkling stars above. Ibrahim probably thought, "Wow, this is way better than a boring day at home!" The people watching were shocked. Their jaws dropped so low, they could have caught butterflies!

As everyone stood there with wide eyes, the king scratched his head in confusion. He had never seen anything like this before! Maybe he thought he needed new glasses, or perhaps he just needed a nap. Ibrahim, still sitting comfortably, waved at the crowd as if to say, "Hey, it's all good! Just chilling here with my buddy Allah!" The people started to whisper among themselves, realizing that Ibrahim was truly special. They began to see that maybe worshiping one God wasn't such a silly idea after all. They were starting to think that Ibrahim was more like a superhero than a troublemaker!

In the end, the king learned a valuable lesson too. He realized that sometimes, the things that seem impossible can actually happen when you have faith. Ibrahim turned the fiery challenge into a tale of bravery, friendship, and the power of believing in something greater than yourself. And from that day on, the people celebrated Ibrahim's courage with a big festival filled with laughter, dancing, and lots of yummy food! They even made a giant bonfire that served as a reminder that love and faith can turn the scariest challenges into the most wonderful adventures. And that's how

Prophet Ibrahim became a hero in the hearts of many!

The Magic of the Moon

Prophet Muhammad and the Splitting Moon

O nce upon a time in a land far away, there lived a very special man named Prophet Muhammad. He was known for his kindness, honesty, and a big heart full of love for everyone. One day, while he was busy sharing stories and teaching people about goodness, something truly amazing happened! The moon, which usually looked like a shiny marble in the night sky, decided it wanted to show off. With a loud "Ka-boom!", it split right in half! Can you imagine the surprise on everyone's faces? It was like the moon was playing peekaboo!

The people gathered around, their eyes wide open and their mouths hanging in disbelief. "Did the moon just do a magic trick?" one curious little boy asked, scratching his head. "I thought only magicians could do that!"

The crowd chuckled, but they were also scratching their heads, wondering how this could happen. Prophet Muhammad smiled at them and said, "Don't worry! It's not magic; it's a sign from Allah!" Everyone nodded, even though they were still trying to wrap their heads around a split moon.

As the two halves of the moon hung in the sky, some people were amazed, while others were not so sure. A few skeptics whispered, "Maybe it's just a big pizza in the sky!" But Prophet Muhammad knew it was a special moment. He encouraged everyone to look at the beauty of Allah's creations and to remember that miracles can happen in the most unexpected ways. And just like that, the moon came back together, and everyone let out a huge sigh of relief, as if the moon had just returned from an exciting adventure!

In the days that followed, stories about the splitting moon spread like wildfire. Kids told their friends at school, "Did you hear about the time the moon got a little too excited and split in half?" They laughed and giggled, imagining the moon on a trampoline, bouncing around. Prophet Muhammad became even more beloved as people realized that he was not just a great teacher, but also a friend who brought joy and wonder into their lives.

So, next time you look up at the moon, remember the story of how it split in half! It's a reminder that amazing things can happen when you have faith and a heart full of love. Just like Prophet Muhammad showed us, we can find joy in the little wonders of life, and who knows? Maybe the moon is just waiting to share another surprise with us! And always remember, it might not just be a big pizza after all!

Nighttime Wonders and Starry Stories

O nce upon a time, in a land where the stars sparkled like diamonds, there lived a curious little boy named Amir. Every night, Amir looked out of his window and wondered about the twinkling stars. "Do they have names? Are they friendly? Can they tell stories?" he pondered. One evening, he decided to climb onto his bed and peek through the telescope his grandfather had given him. He thought if he looked closely enough, he might just catch a star telling a joke or two!

As Amir gazed through the telescope, he spotted a particularly bright star that seemed to dance. "Hey, you up there! Do you know any funny stories?" Amir shouted. To his surprise, the star twinkled back, as if it understood him! Amir chuckled, imagining the star saying, "Why did the sun go to school? To get a little brighter!"

Amir laughed so hard that he nearly fell off his bed. He realized that even the stars could have a sense of humor, just like his friends at school!

Amir thought about the stories his parents told him about the prophets. "I bet they have some nighttime wonders of their own!" he exclaimed. He imagined Prophet Muhammad, peace be upon him, lying under the stars, wondering which star was the biggest and if it ever got tired of shining. Perhaps he even shared a giggle with the moon after telling a funny story about a camel that thought it could dance! Amir's imagination ran wild as he pictured the prophets having starry parties, sharing jokes and laughter just like he did with his friends.

Feeling inspired, Amir decided to create his own bedtime story about the stars and the prophets. He wrote about a magical night when all the prophets gathered under a giant tree, with the stars as their audience. Each prophet took turns telling a story, and the stars would twinkle and shine brighter with every punchline. The audience of stars erupted in laughter when Prophet Jonah told a tale about a fish that was more interested in eating pizza than swimming! Amir giggled at the thought of a fish trying to order a pizza from the underwater restaurant.

As Amir finished his story, he felt a warm glow in his heart. He realized that the nighttime wonders were not just about the stars but also about the stories they could inspire. With a big smile, he whispered, "Good night, stars! Keep shining and telling your stories!" And with that, Amir drifted off to sleep, dreaming of starry gatherings and the laughter of prophets, knowing that every night held a promise of adventure and joy, just waiting for him to discover.

The Super Strong Prophet

Prophet Musa and the Mighty Staff

O nce upon a time, in the land of Egypt, there lived a man named Musa, who was quite special! Musa wasn't just any ordinary guy; he was a prophet chosen by Allah to help his people. Now, Musa had a staff, and oh boy, this wasn't just any stick you'd find in your backyard! This staff was as mighty as a superhero's cape! It could do things that would make even the most powerful magician jealous. Imagine a stick that could turn into a snake! Spoiler alert: it can, and it does!

One sunny day, Musa was feeling a bit nervous about talking to the Pharaoh, the king who thought he was the most powerful person in the land. Musa stood there, holding his staff, and thought, "What if I trip and fall? What if the Pharaoh laughs at me? What if my staff turns into a snake and scares everyone?" Just then, Allah whispered encouragement to him. Musa took a deep breath, and with a swish of his mighty staff, the adventure began! Suddenly, his stick transformed into a slithering snake! Can you imagine the look on the Pharaoh's face? Priceless!

Musa was smart and funny, even when things got serious. He used his cleverness to convince the Pharaoh to let his people go. "Hey, Pharaoh! How about a little magic trick?" Musa said with a cheeky grin. The Pharaoh thought he was the best magician around, but Musa was about to show him that he had some tricks up his sleeve too! With a wave of his staff, he turned the Nile River into blood! "Oops! Looks like someone needs to call a plumber!" Musa chuckled, making sure to lighten the heavy atmosphere.

But the Pharaoh was not amused. He challenged Musa to a show-down! "Bring it on!" he shouted, thinking he could outsmart Musa. So, they gathered all the magicians in Egypt for a competition. The magicians threw their staffs, and they turned into snakes, but

Musa's staff swallowed them all! It was like a snake-eating contest, and Musa's staff was the champion! The crowd cheered, and even the Pharaoh had to admit that Musa was not just a funny guy but also super talented!

Finally, with the help of Allah, Musa led his people out of Egypt, crossing the Red Sea with his mighty staff. Can you imagine walking on dry land while water stood tall on both sides? It was like a water park, but way cooler! Musa was a hero, not just because of his staff, but because he believed in himself and trusted

Allah. So remember, kids, always believe in your own magic, and maybe, just maybe, you'll have your own adventures like Prophet Musa!

Magic Tricks with a Stick!

Once upon a time in a bustling little village, there lived a clever boy named Samir. He was always on the lookout for fun ways to impress his friends, and one sunny afternoon, he stumbled upon a stick lying on the ground. "Hmm," Samir thought, twirling the stick between his fingers, "this could be my magic wand!" With a twinkle in his eye, he decided it was time to show off some spectacular magic tricks.

Samir gathered his friends, Aisha and Bilal, in the park. "Ladies and gentlemen, prepare to be amazed!" he declared, waving the stick dramatically. His first trick was simple: he pretended to pull a rabbit out of the stick. "Abra-cadabra!" he shouted, but as he looked inside, all he found was a very confused ladybug. "Well, that's not a rabbit, but it's a lucky ladybug! Let's call it a magic la-dybug instead!" His friends gig-gled, and the ladybug flitted away, probably wondering what all the fuss was about.

Not one to give up, Samir decided to try something even more daring. He pointed the stick at a nearby tree and proclaimed, "With a swish and a flick, I will make this tree dance!" He began to wiggle the stick and jumped around, making silly dance moves. To his surprise, a gentle breeze rustled the leaves, making it look like the tree was dancing along. "See! The tree loves my magic!" he exclaimed, and Aisha and Bilal clapped and laughed, pretending to join the tree in its dance.

Next, Samir had an idea that was absolutely out of this world. "I will turn this stick into a snake!" he announced enthusiastically. He wrapped the stick in his scarf, making it look long and snaky. "Sssssslither, ssssnake!" he hissed. As he waved his new "snake" around, he accidentally knocked over a flower pot. The flowers tumbled out, and it looked like they were trying to escape the "snake"! Aisha burst into laughter, and Bilal said, "Watch out! The flowers are running away!" It was the funniest moment ever, and Samir decided he was better off with his stick as a magic wand than a snake.

As the sun began to set, Samir realized that the best magic trick of all was the fun and laughter they shared together. "You know," he said, "the real magic comes from friendship and having a good time." Aisha and Bilal nodded in agreement, and they all sat together, enjoying the fading sunlight. Samir smiled, waving his stick one last time. "Let's always remember to find magic in every day, even if it comes from a silly stick!" And with that, they all laughed, knowing that true magic was all around them, especially when they were together.

The Garden of Patience

Prophet Ayyub and His Endless Trials

O nce upon a time, in a land filled with beautiful gardens and singing birds, there lived a man named Ayyub, also known as Job. He was the happiest man in the world, with a big house, a loving family, and more sheep than you could count! Ayyub was known for being super kind and generous, sharing his yummy food and helping anyone in need. If you were in his neighborhood, you'd definitely want to hang out with him, especially if he was grilling some delicious lamb kebabs!

But one day, something strange happened. Just when Ayyub thought his life was perfect, a big storm of troubles started to blow through! First, all his sheep decided they wanted to take a vacation—who knows where they went! Then, his family got sick, and it felt like his whole world was turning upside down. Imagine if your favorite toy went missing, your ice cream melted, and your best friend forgot your birthday all at the same time! That's how Ayyub felt, but instead of crying, he chose to laugh. "Well, if my sheep are on holiday, I hope they're having the time of their lives!"

Ayyub didn't let his troubles get him down. He remembered to be grateful for all the good things he had. He would sit outside, looking at the beautiful sky and thinking about how wonderful the world is. He even started talking to the birds! "Hey there, little buddies! Have you seen my sheep?" The birds would chirp back as if to say, "Not today, Ayyub, but keep smiling!" Ayyub showed everyone that even when life feels like a tricky puzzle, it's essential to keep a happy heart and a cheerful spirit.

As the days turned into weeks, Ayyub faced even more challenges. His friends, who used to love hanging out with him, started to avoid him. They didn't know how to help, so they just stayed away. But guess what? Ayyub didn't get mad! Instead, he made up silly songs about his troubles.

"Oh, my sheep have gone to play; maybe they'll come back some-day!" The funny songs made him giggle, and soon, even the birds were singing along! Ayyub's laughter was so contagious that soon enough, his friends came back, curious about what was making him so jolly.

Finally, after many trials, Ayyub's patience and joy paid off! One day, out of the blue, everything changed. His sheep returned, his family got better, and even the sun seemed to shine brighter! Ayyub realized that the more he smiled through his troubles, the more happiness he found. He became a role model for every-one, teaching them that life may throw challenges our way, but with laughter, kindness, and a sprinkle of patience, we can turn even the toughest days into fun adventures. And from that day on, whenever someone felt sad or lost, they would remember the joyful stories of Ayyub and his endless trials, laughing through every twist and turn of life!

The Treasure of Kindness

Prophet Isa and the Healing Touch

P rophet Isa was known for his amazing ability to heal people, but did you know that he also had a magical touch that could make people giggle? One sunny day, Prophet Isa was walking through a village when he spotted a man whose leg was stuck in a hole. The man was hopping around like a chicken trying to escape! Prophet Isa chuckled and said, "Hold still! I'm coming to save you!" With a gentle touch and a sprinkle of laughter, the man's leg was free, and he danced around, calling Prophet Isa the best doctor in the world!

Now, healing was not just about fixing boo-boos and sore spots for Prophet Isa. He had a special connection with animals too! One day, he found a little bird who had hurt its wing. The bird looked at Prophet Isa with big, sad eyes, as if it was saying, "Help me, please!" Prophet Isa gently picked up the bird, whispered a funny joke about a cat wearing glasses, and, poof! The bird's wing was healed, and it flew away singing silly songs. Everyone in the village laughed and clapped, thinking that Prophet Isa had a magical way of making the world a happier place.

One of the funniest moments in Prophet Isa's healing adventures happened when he met a lady who had a terrible headache. She was lying down and groaning, "Oh, my head!" Prophet Isa approached her and asked, "Have you tried counting how many cookies you can eat without feeling sick?" The lady looked puzzled, but she started counting in her head. While she was distracted, Prophet Isa gave her a light tap on the head. Suddenly, her headache disappeared, and she burst into laughter! "I feel so much better! It must be the cookie magic!" she exclaimed, making everyone giggle.

Prophet Isa also loved to play games with the children in the village. One day, he organized a race where everyone had to hop like bunnies. But here's the twist: each time someone fell, Prophet Isa would heal them with a funny dance move! So, when a child tripped and fell, Prophet Isa would do a silly jig, and the child would laugh so hard that they'd forget they were hurt. The village was filled with joy and laughter, showing how healing could be fun when you added a sprinkle of humor to it.

Prophet Isa's adventures remind us that healing isn't just about fixing what's broken; it's also about bringing smiles and joy to those around us. Whether it was a leg stuck in a hole, a bird with a sore wing, or a lady with a headache, Prophet Isa found a way to make everything better with laughter. So, whenever you feel a little down, remember the funny stories of Prophet Isa and try to find something to laugh about. After all, a good giggle can sometimes be the best medicine!

The Power of a Smile

In a small village filled with colorful houses and friendly animals, there lived a boy named Ahmed. Ahmed had a secret superpower – his smile! It was so bright that it could light up the darkest corners of a room. One day, while playing with his friends, he noticed that Sadia, the shy girl from school, was sitting alone under a tree. Ahmed thought, "Hmm, my smile could help her feel better!" So, he put on his biggest grin and tiptoed over to her. "Hey Sadia, why did the banana go to the doctor? Because it wasn't peeling well!" he exclaimed. With that silly joke, Sadia burst into laughter, and Ahmed's smile became even brighter!

Sadia wasn't the only one who felt the magic of Ahmed's smile. Every time he flashed those pearly whites, it was like spreading sunshine. One sunny afternoon, Ahmed and his friends decided to have a picnic. They packed sandwiches shaped like stars and cookies with funny faces. When they arrived at the park, they saw that the flowers looked droopy, and even the butterflies seemed a little tired. Ahmed thought, "This needs a smile makeover!" So, he started telling jokes about chickens crossing the road and how camels love to wear sunglasses. Soon, the flowers perked up, the butterflies danced around, and even the grumpy old man on the bench cracked a smile!

One day, during a special festival, people were setting up colorful tents and delicious food stalls.

Ahmed noticed that some children looked sad because they didn't have anyone to play with. He decided it was time to unleash his superpower again! He gathered everyone around and said, "Why did the teddy bear say no to dessert? Because it was already stuffed!" The children erupted in giggles, and their faces lit up like fireworks in the night sky. They all joined in, sharing their own funny jokes and stories. The festival became the happiest place on Earth, all thanks to Ahmed's incredible smile!

Now, let's take a moment to think about how a simple smile can change the world. When the Prophet Muhammad, peace be upon him, smiled, it was like he was sending a little piece of joy to everyone around him. Smiling is a way to show kindness, just like giving someone a warm hug or sharing your favorite toy. It's a wonderful gift that costs nothing but can brighten someone's day. Ahmed learned that when he smiled, he was not just making others happy; he was also filling his heart with joy.

So, remember this, young adventurers: your smile is a powerful tool! Just like Ahmed, you can use your smile to spread happiness wherever you go. Whether you're at school, at home, or even during a festival, never forget that a smile can turn a frown upside down. And who knows, maybe one day, you'll be known as the "Smile Superhero" in your own village, just like Ahmed! So go ahead, flash those smiles, share those giggles, and let your joy shine bright!

Celebrating Together

Eid Adventures

Food, Fun, and Friends

E id is one of the most exciting times of the year, and it's not just because of the amazing food! Imagine a day where your house smells like cookies, your friends are bouncing off the walls with excitement, and everyone is wearing their shiniest clothes. That's right! It's time for Eid! On this special day, everyone gathers to celebrate and enjoy all the wonderful things that come with it. There are games to play, delicious dishes to devour, and friends to meet. But be careful—sometimes, the fun can get a little out of hand!

Let's start with the food. Have you ever seen a table filled with so many tasty treats that you thought it might just explode? That's what happens at Eid! There are juicy kebabs, fluffy biryani, sweet cakes, and don't forget the cookies shaped like stars and moons. But wait—what's that? If you're not careful, your little brother might sneak a cookie before you even get a chance to grab one! And then, before you know it, he's trying to do a cookie dance while you're trying to chase him down! Who knew a cookie could cause so much trouble?

Once the food is devoured, it's time for some fun! Picture all the kids running around playing hide and seek, but instead of hiding behind trees, they're hiding behind enormous piles of pillows. Or maybe you and your friends decide to have a water balloon fight! Just be prepared—your mom might not be too happy if she finds a soggy balloon hiding under the couch later. But hey, nothing says "Eid" like a little laughter and a lot of splashes! Just remember, if you get wet, it's all in the name of fun.

Now, let's not forget about the friends! Eid is the perfect time to catch up with your buddies. You can share stories about your favorite toys or even make up silly jokes that make everyone giggle. "Why did the date go to school?" you might ask. "Because it wanted to be a little more a-peeling!"

Get it? But sometimes, the best fun comes from just being silly together. Maybe you and your friends can wear matching hats, create a dance, or even put on a little puppet show with your stuffed animals. The crazier, the better!

As the sun sets and the stars twinkle in the sky, the laughter and joy of Eid fill the air. You might gather around to share stories about the prophets and how they celebrated kindness and friendship. It's a perfect way to end a day full of adventures, food, and fun! And as you snuggle into bed, you can drift off dreaming about the next Eid adventure, wondering what new silly games and tasty treats await you. No matter how you celebrate, remember that the best part of Eid is sharing it with friends and family, making it a day to remember!

Nature's Wonders

The Stories of Creation

In the beginning, long before there were smartphones, video games, or even pizza, there was just a big, empty place. Imagine a giant blank canvas waiting for a fantastic artist to come along and paint a masterpiece. This was the world before Allah created everything. It was dark and quiet, like a library during a nap time. But then, with a wave of His hand, Allah decided it was time to bring the universe to life! And guess what? He started with light. Suddenly, there was brightness everywhere, and it was like someone turned on the biggest lamp in the universe. "Let there be light!" He said, and poof! Light danced around like it was at a party!

Now that the light was shining, Allah thought it would be nice to have a little bit of everything. So, He created the sky and the earth. Imagine the sky as a giant blue blanket spread out above us and the earth as a cozy bed where all the plants and animals could play! Allah really loved nature, so He sprinkled trees, flowers, and rivers all around. If you looked closely, you might even see a squirrel trying to do a backflip off a branch! Allah was pleased with His creation, and He must have chuckled when He saw how the animals were having their own little dance-off in the fields.

But wait, there was more! Allah decided that He needed some special friends to share this beautiful world with. So, He created all the animals! There were fluffy sheep, silly goats, and even some clumsy elephants that had a hard time keeping their balance. Can you imagine an elephant trying to tiptoe through a flower garden? It would be like a giant trying to sneak around on tiptoes, but instead, it would just make things go boom! Not to mention the birds that chirped silly songs, making everyone giggle. Allah loved watching them all play together, and He knew they would need a leader.

Then, Allah created humans, starting with Adam. Adam was

like the first superhero, but instead of a cape, he had a big heart! Allah taught him how to take care of the earth and all the creatures in it. Imagine Adam as the world's first gardener, planting seeds and making sure everyone had enough to eat. And don't forget about Eve, who joined Adam to make the best team ever! They were like the ultimate duo, kind of like peanut butter and jelly, spreading joy and love wherever they went. Together, they explored the beautiful gardens and named all the animals, which must have been hilarious since Adam probably had a few silly names in mind!

As the days went by, Allah watched His creation grow and thrive. From the tiniest ant to the tallest mountain, everything had a purpose. He taught Adam and Eve how to appreciate the beauty around them and to be thankful for all the amazing things they had. Allah wanted them to take care of the world and share their joy with others. So, the next time you see a butterfly fluttering by, or a tree swaying in the breeze, remember that it's all part of the incredible story of creation. And just like Adam and Eve, you too can be a part of this adventure, discovering the wonders of the world and spreading happiness wherever you go!

Fun with Animals

Islamic Teachings

Have you ever seen a cat sneak up on a bird? Or watched a dog chase its own tail? Animals can be so funny! In Islam, we learn that all creatures, big and small, are created by Allah. This means that every time you see a silly animal doing something goofy, like a monkey swinging from a tree or a goat trying to climb a mountain, it's a reminder of how creative and funny Allah is! Just like us, animals have their own personalities. Some are curious, some are playful, and some are just plain silly!

Did you know that our Prophet Muhammad, peace be upon him, loved animals? He had a special bond with them and treated them with kindness. There's a story about a cat named Muezza who was so special to him that he would let her sleep on his lap! Imagine having a furry friend that you love so much! One day, when Muezza needed to get down, instead of waking her up, the Prophet cut his sleeve to let her sleep peacefully. Now that's a catnap taken to the next level!

Animals also teach us important lessons. When we watch a bird build its nest or a bee buzzing around collecting nectar, we can learn about hard work and teamwork. Just like bees work together to make honey, we can work together to help our friends and family. And when we see a dog wagging its tail, it reminds us to be happy and spread joy wherever we go! So, the next time you see an animal doing something funny, think about what you can learn from it.

In Islam, we are taught to be gentle and caring toward animals. Whether it's feeding a hungry cat or giving water to a thirsty dog, every little act of kindness counts. There's even a story about a man who gave water to a thirsty dog, and Allah rewarded him for his good deed. So remember, being kind to animals is not just nice; it's also a way to earn Allah's love! Plus, who wouldn't want to be known as the kid who loves animals?

Next time you visit the park or your backyard, keep an eye out for the funny animals around you. Maybe a squirrel will steal your snack or a bird will sing you a silly song! Animals are everywhere, bringing laughter and joy. And as you explore the wonderful world of animals, remember that each one is a sign of Allah's creativity. So go ahead, share a giggle with a goofy creature, and celebrate the fun of Allah's creation!

The Journey of Faith

Little Steps with Big Prophets

Once upon a time, in a land filled with wonder and magic, there lived a group of amazing prophets. They were like superheroes but without capes! Each prophet had a special story to tell, and their adventures were filled with lessons about kindness, bravery, and faith. One day, a curious little boy named Ali decided he wanted to learn more about these prophets. He thought, "If I can learn their stories, maybe I can be a superhero too!" So, he put on his favorite cape (which was really just a towel) and set off on an adventure of his own.

Ali started with Prophet Noah, who built a giant ark. Imagine trying to convince your friends that you're going to build a boat big enough for all the animals in the world! Noah didn't just gather animals; he also had to deal with some rather silly ones. Can you picture a giraffe trying to fit through a tiny door? Or a lion sneezing because of the dust? Ali giggled as he thought about how Noah must have laughed too, reminding himself that sometimes, big tasks can start with little steps, like gathering two of every animal—one step at a time!

Next, Ali learned about Prophet Ibrahim, who had the biggest heart. One day, he was told to sacrifice something he loved dearly. Can you imagine Ibrahim's surprise when he realized it was his beloved camel, named Humpy?

Humpy was the laziest camel around, always falling asleep in the sun. But Ibrahim was brave and showed trust in Allah. Ali thought, "Wow, if Ibrahim can be brave with Humpy, then I can be brave when I have to try new things, like tasting broccoli!"

Then came the story of Prophet Musa, who had a talking stick! Wait, not just any stick—a magical staff that could turn into a snake! Ali couldn't help but laugh at the thought of Musa waving his stick around, surprising everyone. Imagine if you had a stick like that! You could use it to get out of chores by saying, "Sorry, I can't help with the dishes; my snake stick needs some exercise!" Musa's adventures taught Ali that even the smallest things, like a simple stick, can be used to do great things when you believe and have faith.

Finally, Ali heard about Prophet Muhammad, who showed everyone how to share and care. He loved celebrating special days like Eid with friends and family, and he always made sure to include everyone. Ali thought about how much fun it would be to celebrate Eid with a giant cake shaped like a moon! He imagined everyone laughing and sharing stories, just like the prophets did. Ali realized that no matter how small his actions might seem, like sharing a toy or a snack, they could make someone's day a lot brighter. Little steps, just like those taken by the prophets, could lead to big smiles and even bigger adventures!

Growing Strong Through Tough Times

When life gives you lemons, what do you do? You make lemon juice, of course! But what if those lemons are actually giant, talking lemons trying to roll you down a hill? In our adventures, we learn that tough times can sometimes feel like a wild roller-coaster ride. Just like the prophets who faced challenges, we can find ways to grow stronger and even laugh a little along the way. Picture Prophet Job, who had a skin condition and lost everything. Instead of throwing a pity party, he stayed positive. If Job can stay cheerful with a skin condition, then surely we can giggle through our own little bumps in the road!

Imagine being out in the woods, and suddenly it starts pouring rain. You could run for cover, or you could do what our buddy Noah did—build a giant boat!

Noah didn't just sit there and grumble about the weather; he got busy, gathered animals, and made the best of a soggy situation. Maybe next time your little brother spills juice on your favorite book, instead of sulking, you could pretend to be a ship captain navigating through a wild ocean! Remember, every challenge can turn into a fun adventure if you use your imagination.

Do you know the story of Prophet Moses? He faced a pretty big challenge when he had to part the Red Sea. Imagine standing there, looking at a massive wall of water on one side and a group of cranky people on the other! Instead of panicking, he listened to Allah and took action. Sometimes, we might feel like we are stuck in a sticky jam, but just like Moses, we can find our way through it. Maybe you can think of a problem as a big sea that you need to cross. With a little faith and creativity, you can make it to the other side!

Even when things get tough, we can also find strength in our friends and family. Just like how Prophet Muhammad had his friends, the companions, to help him spread kindness and good-ness. Imagine having a superhero squad of your own! When you're feeling down, why not gather your friends and have a laughter par-ty? Share silly stories, play games, and remind each other that to-gether, you can face any chal-lenge. After all, even superheroes need sidekicks to save the day!

In the end, tough times are like the rough patches on a roller-coaster. They might feel a bit scary at first, but when you hold on tight and enjoy the ride, you come out with a big smile on your face. Remember the stories of the prophets and how they grew stronger through their challenges. So, the next time you're faced with a giant lemon or a surprise rainstorm, just think of it as your own adventure. And who knows? You might just discover a whole new way to be brave and have a blast!

Your Own Adventure

Be a Prophet Helper!

Have you ever thought about what it would be like to be a helper for a prophet? Imagine getting to hang out with someone super important, like Prophet Muhammad or Prophet Musa! These prophets were like the superheroes of their time, spreading messages of kindness, faith, and lots of wisdom. But every superhero needs a trusty sidekick, and that's where you come in! Buckle up, because it's time for your own adventure—becoming a Prophet Helper!

First, let's set the scene. You're in the desert, and it's hot—like, really hot! You've got your trusty water bottle and a snack (because heroes need snacks). You're helping Prophet Musa, who always seems to need a hand. "Hey, buddy, can you help me part this sea?" he asks. You nod, excited but also a bit nervous. With a big wave of your hand and a sprinkle of imagination, you help him part the sea like a magic trick! Fish swim by, and you can't help but giggle as they give you a little wave. "You're the best helper ever!" Musa says, and you feel like the coolest kid in the whole wide world.

Now, imagine you're flying through the skies with Prophet Muhammad on a magical carpet. You both zoom past fluffy clouds and do loops around the moon. "Let's spread some kindness down below!" he says. You throw down little notes that say, "Be kind!" and "Share your toys!"

Suddenly, kids everywhere start smiling and sharing their crayons and snacks. You can see them high-fiving each other, and it feels like you're throwing the biggest party ever! "You're a fantastic helper!" Muhammad cheers, and your heart fills with joy as you realize how easy it is to spread happiness.

But wait, it's not all fun and games! Sometimes, you might have to face challenges, like a giant, grumpy camel who doesn't want to share his sand! "What do we do?" you ask Prophet Ibrahim, who's preparing to build a beautiful house for everyone. "Let's make him laugh," he replies with a twinkle in his eye. You start making silly faces and telling jokes about camels. Before you know it, the grumpy camel is rolling on the sand, laughing so hard that he decides to help you build the house instead! It's a reminder that laughter and kindness can solve even the grumpiest problems.

At the end of your adventure, you return home, your heart brimming with stories. You've helped prophets, made friends with fish and camels, and learned that being a helper is all about spreading joy and doing good. Just like the prophets, you can be a little light in the world. So, whenever you see someone who needs a friend, remember that your actions can be just as heroic. Now grab your cape (or a towel), and get ready to be the best prophet helper you can be! Your adventure is just beginning!

The End... or is it?

Well, young adventurer, here we are—the final page of Adventures with the Prophets: Stories for Young Hearts. Can you believe it? You've traveled across stormy seas, sailed on giant arks, hung out with talking birds, and even spent some questionable time in a fish's belly. If books had passports, yours would be stamped with stories from Nineveh, Egypt, and beyond. And honestly, you deserve a snack break.

Go ahead, grab a cookie. I'll wait.

Back? Great! Now, here's the thing about stories like these—they never really end. Sure, the book might close, but these tales have a sneaky way of sticking with you. The next time you see the moon shining bright, you might think of Prophet Muhammad's moon-splitting miracle. When you spot a bird perched on a branch, you might wonder if it's gossiping with Prophet Suleiman. And if you ever (and I mean ever) smell fish sticks for dinner... well, let's just say you might have a little Jonah flashback.

But these stories aren't just here to make you laugh, gasp, or raise your eyebrows so high they touch your hairline—they're also packed with some pretty big lessons. Lessons about being kind, brave, patient, and, most importantly, trusting in something bigger than yourself. (Also, lesson number one: always listen when someone tells you, "Hey, don't hop on that boat to nowhere.")

Now, before we say goodbye, let's make one thing clear: YOU are part of this adventure too. That's right! You may not have a magical staff, an ark full of animals, or a moon that splits in two at your command, but you've got something even cooler—a heart full of kindness and a brain full of ideas. So whether you're helping a friend, being brave in a tricky situation, or simply sharing your snacks (yes, even the last cookie counts), you're already following in the footsteps of some pretty amazing people.

And who knows? Maybe one day, someone will write your story in a book just like this one. "Once upon a time, there was a kid who was so brave, so clever, and so snack-savvy that they became a hero in their own right." Sound good?

Alright, it's time to close this book, but don't worry—it's not really goodbye. These stories will always be here, ready to be reread, giggled over, and shared with others. And hey, if you ever feel like you're stuck in a fishy situation (metaphorically or literally), just remember: every big adventure starts with a small step... and sometimes a really big fish.

Now go on, adventurer. The world is waiting, and so are your next stories. Until then—stay curious, stay kind, and maybe keep an eye out for any unusually large fish in your bathtub.

The end. (Or... the beginning?)

Let's Meet Psalm

Psalm Carnoustie is a passionate children's author dedicated to introducing young readers to the vibrant world of cultures, religions, and timeless wisdom from around the globe. With a warm and engaging storytelling style, Psalm crafts tales that spark curiosity, foster understanding, and celebrate diversity.

Believing that children are the seeds of a more compassionate future, Psalm is driven by the philosophy that early exposure to different beliefs and traditions nurtures empathy, kindness, and open-mindedness. Her books serve as gentle guides, helping children see the beauty in differences while embracing the common threads that unite us all.

When she's not weaving enchanting stories, Psalm enjoys exploring cultural festivals, collecting folklore from faraway lands, and sharing moments of quiet reflection in nature. Her stories are not just books—they are bridges, connecting little hearts to a world of understanding and acceptance.